I0411708

September 2014

DEFENSE PLANNING

DOD Needs Specific Measures and Milestones to Gauge Progress of Preparations for Operational Access Challenges

GAO-14-801

GAO Highlights

Highlights of GAO-14-801, a report to congressional committees

DEFENSE PLANNING

DOD Needs Specific Measures and Milestones to Gauge Progress of Preparations for Operational Access Challenges

Why GAO Did This Study

According to DOD, its ability to deploy military forces from the United States to a conflict area is being increasingly challenged as potential adversaries pursue capabilities designed to deny access. Access can be denied by either preventing an opposing force from entering an operational area or limiting an opposing force's freedom of action within an operational area. DOD has a joint concept that broadly describes how DOD will operate effectively in such access-denied environments. DOD's initial efforts have emphasized the roles of the Air Force and Navy.

GAO was mandated to review the role of the Army and Marine Corps in access-denied areas. This report (1) describes Army and Marine Corps efforts to address operational access challenges and (2) analyzes the extent to which DOD is able to gauge how its efforts support implementation of its concept for future operations in access-denied environments. GAO analyzed DOD, Army, and Marine Corps concepts; reports on service-level exercises; DOD policy and guidance on concept implementation; and documents specifically related to the joint concept. GAO also interviewed cognizant DOD officials.

What GAO Recommends

GAO recommends that DOD establish specific measures and milestones in future iterations of the JOAC Implementation Plan to improve DOD's ability to gauge implementation progress. DOD agreed with the importance of assessing the plan and said it is developing measures and milestones and will continue to refine these tracking tools in the future.

View GAO-14-801. For more information, contact John Pendleton at (202) 512-3489 or pendletonj@gao.gov .

What GAO Found

The Army and Marine Corps are undertaking multiple efforts to address operational access challenges—challenges that impede a military force's ability to enter and conduct operations in an area—that impact a broad range of their existing missions. For example, they are incorporating operational access challenges into their wargames and revising their service concepts, which inform their assessments of capability needs, gaps, and solutions. In addition, the Army and the Marine Corps have identified important roles they play in overcoming operational access challenges and are examining ways to carry them out in access-denied environments, including

- engagement activities—improving access conditions through such activities as multinational exercises, prepositioning supplies, and forward presence, and

- entry operations—deploying forces onto foreign territory to conduct missions such as eliminating land-based threats to access.

In addition, the Army has identified areas specific to its role, including

- logistics—sustaining forces despite increased vulnerabilities from access threats and challenges associated with new operational approaches, and

- missile defense—providing defense against increasingly accurate, lethal, and available ballistic and cruise missiles.

The Department of Defense (DOD) is unable to gauge the extent to which its efforts to overcome operational access challenges support the implementation of the 2012 *Joint Operational Access Concept* (JOAC). The JOAC describes how the department will operate effectively in future operating environments with access challenges and is intended to guide the development of capabilities for the joint force of 2020. The Joint Staff is leading a multiyear DOD-wide effort, initiated in June 2013, to coordinate, oversee, and assess the department's implementation of the JOAC. DOD plans to issue the first iteration of the JOAC Implementation Plan in 2014 and to assess and update the plan annually. The draft plan focuses on the highest-priority JOAC-required capabilities and identifies related actions, but does not fully establish specific measures and milestones to gauge progress. While DOD has stated its intent to assess progress in the future, its current planning lacks specific details about the measures it will employ and the milestones it will use to gauge that progress. Until DOD establishes specific measures and milestones in future iterations of its implementation plan, the department will not be able to gauge implementation progress and assess whether efforts by the joint force, to include the Army and the Marine Corps, will achieve DOD's goals in desired time frames. As a result, DOD may lack assurance that efforts, including those currently being undertaken by the Army and the Marine Corps to address areas such as engagement activities, entry operations, logistics, and expeditionary missile defense, will fully align with the JOAC.

_____ United States Government Accountability Office

Contents

Letter		1
	Background	4
	Army and Marine Corps Are Undertaking Efforts to Prepare for Operational Access Challenges	10
	DOD Is in the Early Stages of Developing the JOAC Implementation Plan, but Has Not Fully Established Specific Measures and Milestones to Assess Progress	19
	Conclusions	25
	Recommendation for Executive Action	26
	Agency Comments and Our Evaluation	27

Appendix I	Joint Operational Access Concept Required Capabilities	30

Appendix II	Comments from the Department of Defense	33

Appendix III	GAO Contact and Staff Acknowledgments	35

Figures		
	Figure 1: Examples of Anti-Access and Area Denial Capabilities	5
	Figure 2: Range of Anti-Access/Area Denial Challenges	6
	Figure 3: Strategic Guidance and Concepts That Address Operational Access Challenges	9
	Figure 4: Focus of Army and Marine Corps Wargame Scenarios	12
	Figure 5: Draft 2014 Joint Operational Access Concept Implementation Plan Measures and Milestones	24

Abbreviations

A2/AD	anti-access/area denial
CENTCOM	U.S. Central Command
CJCSI	Chairman of the Joint Chiefs of Staff Instruction
DOD	Department of Defense
DODD	Department of Defense Directive
JOAC	*Joint Operational Access Concept*
PACOM	U.S. Pacific Command
QDR	Quadrennial Defense Review

GAO U.S. GOVERNMENT ACCOUNTABILITY OFFICE

441 G St. N.W.
Washington, DC 20548

September 10, 2014

Congressional Committees

For decades, the Department of Defense's (DOD) ability to deploy military forces from the United States to a conflict area went essentially unopposed. For example, U.S. and coalition forces flowed into the Persian Gulf area unhindered for 6 months in the buildup to Operation Desert Storm in 1990 and 1991. However, this global reach is being increasingly challenged with potential adversaries now pursuing anti-access/area denial (A2/AD) strategies and capabilities designed to either prevent an opposing force from entering an operational area (anti-access) or limit an opposing force's freedom of action within an operational area (area denial), according to DOD. For instance, potential adversaries could challenge DOD's ability to deploy military forces by using ballistic and cruise missiles to prevent U.S. forces from getting to an operational area by attacking U.S. bases, ships, and logistics hubs. Similarly, potential adversaries could use mines and guided rockets to limit U.S. freedom of action once U.S. forces are in an area. DOD is increasingly focusing on A2/AD challenges and issued the *Joint Operational Access Concept* (JOAC) in 2012,[1] which broadly describes how it will operate effectively in an A2/AD environment to support development of the joint force of 2020, as described by the 2012 Defense Strategic Guidance.[2]

We issued two classified reports in 2013 focused on the A2/AD capabilities of Iran and China and DOD's ability to overcome them. A House Armed Services Committee report accompanying the National Defense Authorization Act for Fiscal Year 2014 noted that DOD's initial efforts to prepare for A2/AD challenges emphasized the roles of the Air Force and Navy in countering A2/AD challenges, while less attention has

---

[1]Joint Chiefs of Staff, *Joint Operational Access Concept* (JOAC) (Washington, D.C.: Jan. 17, 2012). Within DOD, joint concepts link strategic guidance to the development and employment of future joint force capabilities. A primary purpose of concepts is to propose new approaches for current or future challenges and provide guidance for future force development. Concepts, which are developed and refined through things such as wargames, studies, and exercises, serve as a basis for determining requirements for the future force and informing capability assessments and resource decisions.

[2]Department of Defense, *Sustaining U.S. Global Leadership: Priorities for 21st Century Defense,* (Washington, D.C.: January 2012). In this report, we refer to this guidance as the 2012 Defense Strategic Guidance.

GAO-14-801 Defense Planning

been given to the roles of the Army and Marine Corps.[3] Further, the committee's report mandated us to review the role of the Army and Marine Corps in access-denied environments. This report (1) describes Army and Marine Corps efforts to address operational access challenges and (2) analyzes the extent to which DOD is able to gauge how its efforts support implementation of its concept for future operations in an access-denied environment.

To describe Army and Marine Corps efforts to address operational access challenges, we reviewed and analyzed documents from both services. These included the *Army Capstone Concept*, the *Army Operating Concept* (draft), and the *Marine Corps' Expeditionary Force 21–Forward and Ready: Now and in the Future*; reports and briefings on service-level wargames and exercises; studies and reviews of possible future operations in A2/AD environments conducted or sponsored by DOD; and other documents describing ideas or initiatives for how Army and Marine Corps forces might overcome A2/AD challenges.

To analyze the extent to which DOD is able to gauge how its efforts support implementation of its concept for future operations in an access-denied environment, we reviewed and analyzed DOD strategic guidance, including the 2012 Defense Strategic Guidance and the 2014 Quadrennial Defense Review,[4] and joint concepts that discuss the implications of operations in A2/AD environments, such as the *Joint Operational Access Concept*, the *Air-Sea Battle Concept*, and the *Joint Concept for Entry Operations*. We also reviewed and analyzed DOD's policies and guidance on concept implementation and its specific plans for implementation of the JOAC, including the Joint Operational Access Implementation Terms of Reference and a draft of the implementation plan being developed by DOD during the time of our review. We used criteria based on DOD guidance for concept implementation, DOD's JOAC implementation guidance, standards for internal control in the

---

[3]See H. Rep. No. 113-102 (June 7, 2013) accompanying H.R. 1960, a bill for the National Defense Authorization Act for Fiscal Year 2014.

[4]Section 118 of Title 10 of the United States Code requires the Secretary of Defense to conduct a comprehensive examination of the national defense strategy, force structure, force modernization plans, infrastructure, budget plan, and other elements of the defense program and policies of the United States, every 4 years, with a view toward determining and expressing the nation's defense strategy and establishing a defense program for the next 20 years.

federal government, and best practices for developing project schedules to assess DOD's implementation plan for the JOAC.[5]

For both objectives, we interviewed DOD officials to gain a better understanding of how DOD and the services are taking steps to address operations in A2/AD environments and the extent to which DOD is positioned to integrate those efforts into its DOD-wide implementation of its concept for future operations in A2/AD environments. Specifically, we interviewed officials from the Office of the Under Secretary of Defense for Policy; Office of the Under Secretary of Defense for Acquisition, Technology, and Logistics; Air Sea Battle Office; Joint Staff; Army Capabilities Integration Command; Marine Corps Combat Development Command; and Army officials with logistics and missile defense expertise. On the basis of discussions with DOD officials, we also met with officials from U.S. Pacific Command, U.S. Central Command, U.S. Special Operations Command, and U.S. Transportation Command.

We conducted this performance audit from July 2013 to September 2014 in accordance with generally accepted government auditing standards. Those standards require that we plan and perform the audit to obtain sufficient, appropriate evidence to provide a reasonable basis for our findings and conclusions based on our audit objectives. We believe that the evidence obtained provides a reasonable basis for our findings and conclusions based on our audit objectives.

---

[5]GAO, *Standards for Internal Control in the Federal Government*, GAO/AIMD-00-21.3.1 (Washington, D.C.: Nov. 1, 1999), and *Schedule Assessment Guide: Best Practices for Project Schedules*, GAO-12-120G (exposure draft), (Washington, D.C.: May 2012). The GAO *Schedule Assessment Guide* provides 10 best practices to help managers and auditors ensure that the program schedule is reliable and evaluate the economy, efficiency, and effectiveness of government programs. The 10 best practices, developed with help from experts from the scheduling community, further develop the concepts introduced in our *Cost Estimating and Assessment Guide*. See GAO, *Cost Estimating and Assessment Guide: Best Practices for Developing and Managing Capital Program Costs*, GAO-093SP (Washington, D.C: Mar. 2, 2009).

Background

Future Operational Environment Includes Increasing A2/AD Challenges

Future A2/AD challenges are part of a security environment that will be characterized by increasing complexity, uncertainty, and rapid change, according to DOD. Further, national security challenges will continue to arise from ongoing concerns such as violent extremism, the proliferation of weapons of mass destruction, resource competition, and the rise of modern competitor states, among others. These concerns, according to DOD, combined with the proliferation of advanced technologies; the increasing importance of space and cyberspace; and the ubiquity of digital networks, including social media, will make the future security environment less predictable, more complex, and potentially more dangerous than it is today.

The JOAC notes that challenges to operational access are not new but that three trends promise to significantly complicate DOD's ability to establish operational access.[6] According to the JOAC, the three trends are

- *Technology Improvement and Proliferation:* The first important trend is the dramatic improvement and proliferation of weapons and other technologies capable of denying access or freedom of action within an operational area. Specifically, an increasing number of state and nonstate actors are developing or obtaining weapons of increasing range and accuracy.

- *Space and Cyberspace Emergence*: The second and related trend is the emergence of space and cyberspace as increasingly important and contested domains. According to the JOAC, the U.S. military will continue to derive great benefit from its space and cyberspace capabilities, but potential adversaries understand that and are increasingly targeting those capabilities. Operating in the space and cyberspace domains is also attractive to potential adversaries because actions in those domains are often difficult to attribute.

- *Posture Changes:* The third trend is that the change in U.S. overseas defense posture complicates the U.S. ability to obtain operational

---

[6]The JOAC defines operational access as the ability to project military force into an operational area with sufficient freedom of action to accomplish the mission. In this report, we use operational access challenges to refer to both anti-access and area denial.

access. Specifically, DOD has reduced the number of overseas facilities and number of deployed forces, meaning that future operations will likely require it to deploy over longer distances.

According to the JOAC, the effect of these three trends is that potential adversaries who may have once perceived that they could not stop U.S. forces from deploying into an operational area are now adopting A2/AD strategies. Figure 1 provides examples of anti-access and area denial capabilities.

Figure 1: Examples of Anti-Access and Area Denial Capabilities

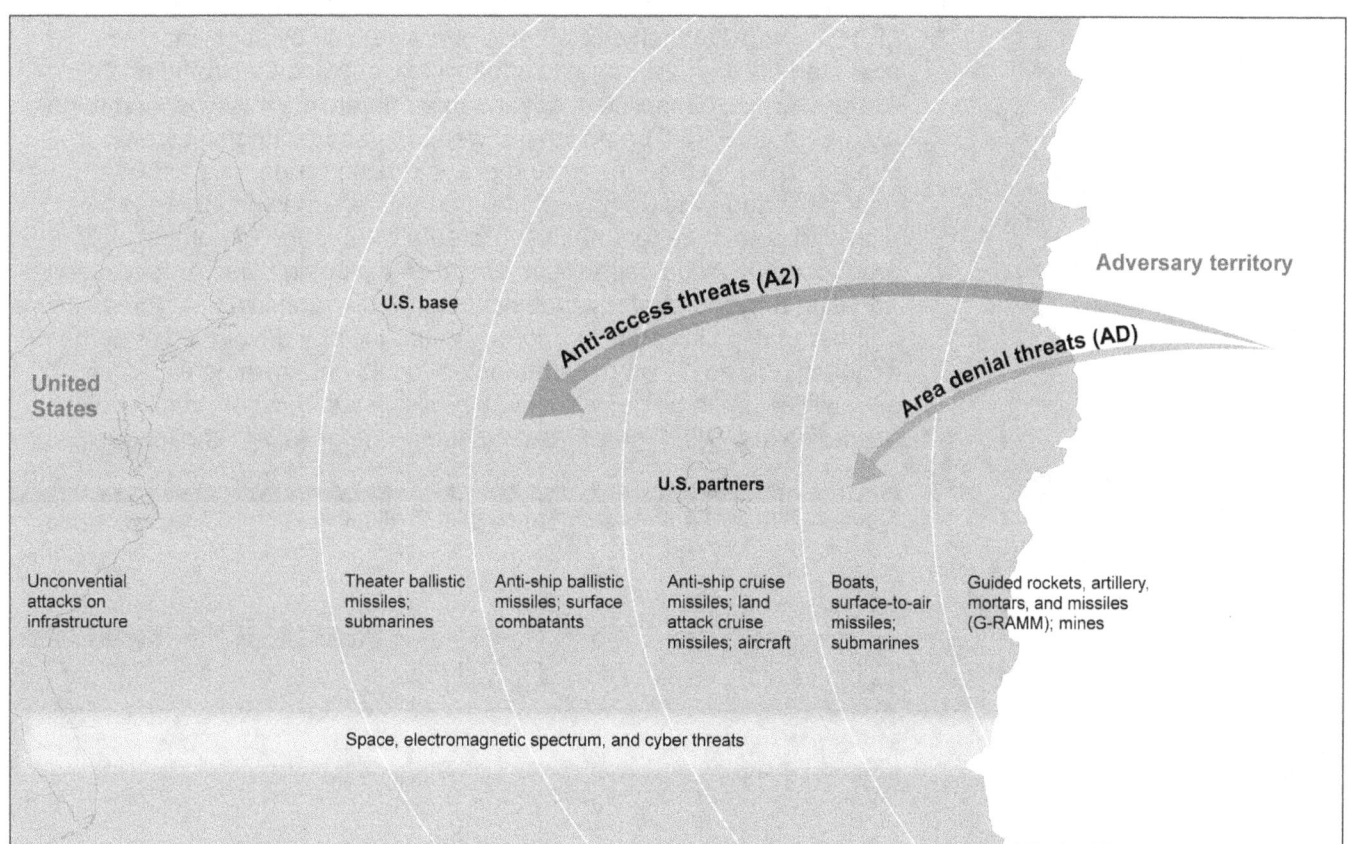

Note: Notional map.

The JOAC describes A2/AD challenges in the context of an adversary's strategy rather than a list of technical capabilities that need to be overcome. In general, the intent of an adversary that adopts an A2/AD strategy is to convince and, if necessary and possible, compel the United States to keep out of its affairs. At the most sophisticated level, an A2/AD strategy is not a sequential series of actions using specific military capabilities but rather an integrated and adaptive campaign using all levers of national power and influence before, during, and after any actual military conflict. Critical elements of an A2/AD strategy include keeping U.S. forces as far away as possible and imposing steeper costs on the United States than it is willing to bear.

Militarily, an A2/AD environment is characterized by sophisticated adversaries using asymmetric capabilities, such as electronic and cyber warfare, space capabilities, advanced air defenses, missiles, and mines, according to DOD. The advanced weapons and technologies are characterized by their increasing precision and range, and are often affordable and increasingly proliferated. Adversaries could range from a high-end peer state that has integrated a wide range of domestically produced advanced capabilities to states, including failed or failing states, adopting a hybrid strategy that includes regular and irregular forces and a number of sophisticated weapons and technology developed at home or acquired abroad. Even nonstate actors could obtain some A2/AD capabilities, such as guided anti-ship missiles and cyber attack tools, according to DOD. Figure 2 depicts the range of A2/AD challenges.

Figure 2: Range of Anti-Access/Area Denial Challenges

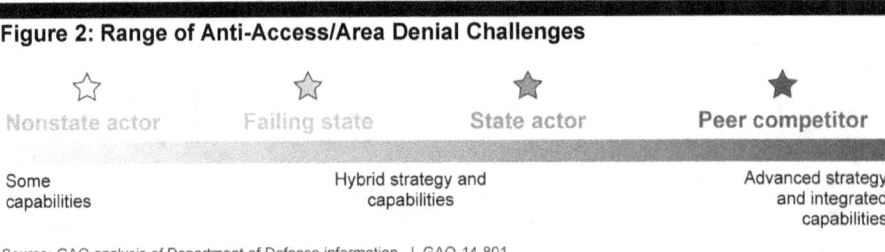

Source: GAO analysis of Department of Defense information. | GAO-14-801
Note: Not to scale.

DOD Strategic Guidance and Recent Joint Concepts Focus on Operational Access

DOD has increasingly focused over the past few years on the operational access challenges it may face in the future, although it has recognized A2/AD challenges for well over a decade. For example, *projecting and sustaining U.S. forces in distant A2/AD environments and defeating A2/AD threats* was one of six operational goals identified in the 2001 Quadrennial Defense Review (QDR). However, DOD's focus over the subsequent decade was on operations in Afghanistan and Iraq. As those operations began to wind down, DOD began to reemphasize the need to be able to overcome challenges to operational access.

The 2012 Defense Strategic Guidance was intended to transition the department from an emphasis on current operations to preparing for future challenges, including helping guide decisions regarding the size and shape of the future force in a more fiscally constrained environment.[7] In the guidance, the Secretary of Defense established *projecting power despite A2/AD challenges* as 1 of 10 primary DOD missions, noting that countries such as Iran and China will continue to pursue capabilities such as electronic and cyber warfare and ballistic and cruise missiles to counter U.S. power projection capabilities and limit the operational access of U.S. forces. Other primary missions, such as operating effectively in cyberspace and space, deterring and defeating aggression, and providing a stabilizing presence, are also relevant to overcoming A2/AD challenges.

The 2014 QDR maintains the emphasis on overcoming A2/AD challenges. It builds on the 2012 Defense Strategic Guidance and continues DOD's transition to focusing on future challenges during a time of fiscal uncertainty. The QDR states that DOD must be prepared for a full range of conflicts, including against state powers with advanced A2/AD capabilities. Further, two of the QDR's three strategic pillars—*build security globally* and *project power and win decisively*—emphasize the importance of being able to project power and overcome challenges to access. The 2014 QDR also stresses that innovation will be paramount across all of DOD's activities in order to best address the increasingly complex operational environment.

The Chairman of the Joint Chiefs of Staff has also issued guidance in the past 2 years that emphasizes the importance of overcoming access challenges. *The Capstone Concept for Joint Operations: Joint Force 2020* is the foundational concept document that describes the Chairman's vision for how the joint force will defend the nation against a wide range of security challenges and helps establish force development priorities.[8]

---

[7]DOD, *Sustaining U.S. Global Leadership: Priorities for 21st Century Defense* (Washington, D.C.: January 2012). In this report, we refer to this guidance as the 2012 Defense Strategic Guidance.

[8]Joint Chiefs of Staff, *Capstone Concept for Joint Operations: Joint Force 2020* (Washington, D.C.: Sept. 10, 2012).

Among these priorities is developing capabilities to defeat A2/AD threats, which as noted above is the specific focus of the JOAC.

The JOAC includes a list of 30 required capabilities that are essential to the implementation of the concept (see app. I). It further states that this list is neither complete nor prioritized but provides a baseline for further analysis and concept development. DOD also has a number of supporting concepts to the JOAC that provide further detail on specific aspects of operations in A2/AD environments. The first of these supporting concepts is the *Air-Sea Battle Concept*, which is focused on overcoming the longer-range and advanced anti-access challenges.[9] At the direction of the Secretary of Defense, the Departments of the Navy and Air Force developed this multiservice concept focused on gaining and maintaining freedom of action in the global commons, that is, the areas of air, sea, space, and cyberspace that belong to no one state.[10] In April 2014, the Chairman of the Joint Chiefs of Staff issued the *Joint Concept for Entry Operations*, a supporting concept to JOAC focused on how forces will enter onto foreign territory and immediately conduct operations in the face of adversaries with increasingly effective area-denial strategies and capabilities. There are a number of other existing concepts, as well as concepts that are being developed, that support the JOAC (see fig. 3).

---

[9]DOD, *Air-Sea Battle Concept* (Washington, D.C.: June 2, 2011).

[10]The Air-Sea Battle Concept is a multiservice supporting concept, rather than a joint supporting concept. The Air-Sea Battle Office was created in November 2011 by the Navy and the Air Force—later expanded to include the Army and Marine Corps, pursuant to an August 2012 joint memorandum—in order to implement the Air-Sea Battle Concept.

Figure 3: Strategic Guidance and Concepts That Address Operational Access Challenges

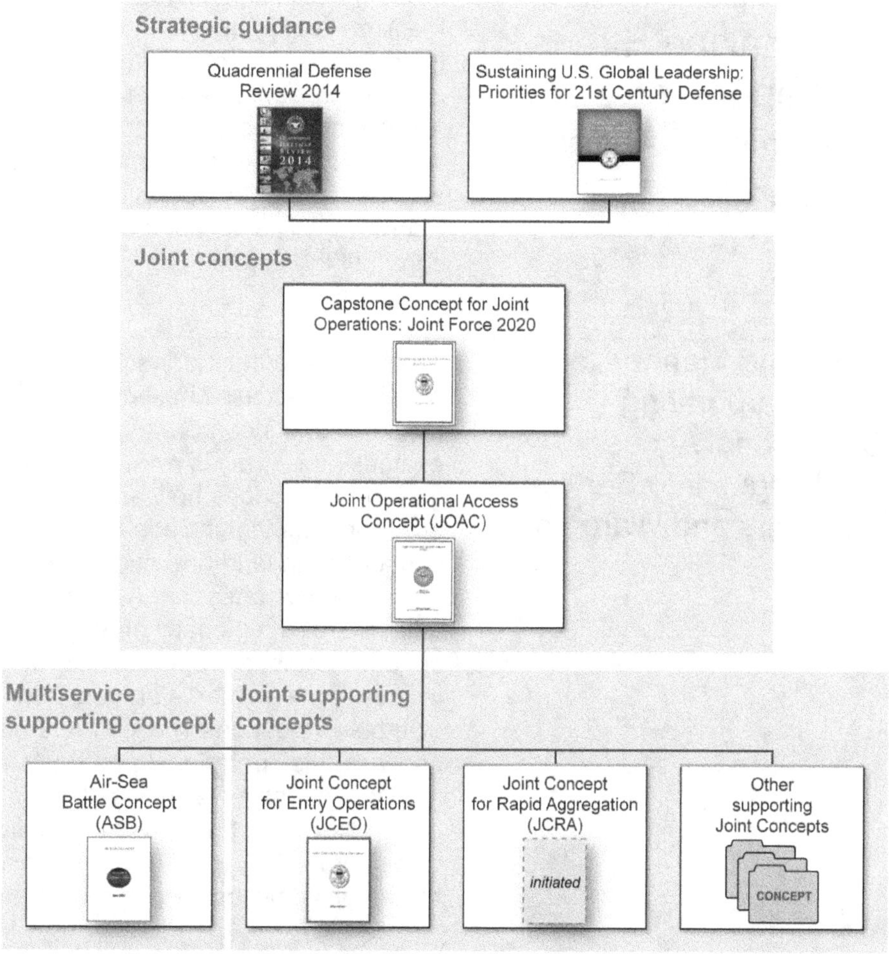

Strategic guidance

Quadrennial Defense
Review 2014

Sustaining U.S. Global Leadership:
Priorities for 21st Century Defense

Joint concepts

Capstone Concept for Joint
Operations: Joint Force 2020

Joint Operational Access
Concept (JOAC)

Multiservice
supporting concept

Joint supporting
concepts

Air-Sea
Battle Concept
(ASB)

Joint Concept
for Entry Operations
(JCEO)

Joint Concept
for Rapid Aggregation
(JCRA)

initiated

Other
supporting
Joint Concepts

CONCEPT

Source: GAO analysis of Department of Defense information. | GAO-14-801

Note: Department of Defense (DOD) concepts propose new approaches for current or future challenges and provide guidance for future force development.

Army and Marine Corps Are Undertaking Efforts to Prepare for Operational Access Challenges

The Army and Marine Corps are undertaking multiple efforts to address operational access challenges, which impact a broad range of their existing missions. In light of the rapidly changing operational environment, the Army and Marine Corps are reviewing how they will need to carry out their roles and functions in part by revising their service concepts and by conducting wargames that incorporate such challenges. Further, the Army and Marine Corps have identified several areas where they have important roles in overcoming access challenges, including engagement activities and entry operations, as well as logistics and missile defense for the Army.[11] The services are beginning to take steps to change how they carry out these roles.

Army and Marine Corps Are Incorporating Operational Access Challenges into Service Concepts and Wargames

The Army and the Marine Corps have begun examining the impact of operational access challenges on existing missions by revising their concepts and incorporating such challenges into their wargames. For example, the Army is revising the *Army Operating Concept*, which generally describes how an Army commander will operate in future environments that include A2/AD challenges, and identifies required capabilities in land operations. Given future operational challenges, the draft concept states that Army forces need to be agile, responsive, adaptive, and regionally engaged across the globe, and be able to conduct distributed operations. These distributed operations would involve Army elements arriving from numerous directions and domains to distributed locations in a joint operations area. According to the draft concept, this operational approach, also discussed in the JOAC, could help to overcome A2/AD challenges because the Army forces would be more spread out and thus more difficult to target and defend against. Once completed, the *Army Operating Concept* is to provide guidance for the Army's development of supporting functional concepts, which

---

[11]Department of Defense Directive (DODD) 5100.01, *Functions of the Department of Defense and its Major Components*, (Dec. 21, 2010) (hereinafter cited as DODD 5100.01 [Dec. 21, 2010]) states that all of the services have responsibilities to organize, train, and equip forces for offensive and defensive cyberspace operations. It also states that the Army has responsibility to provide support for space operations to enhance joint campaigns in coordination with the other military services. The JOAC identifies the emergence of space and cyberspace as increasingly important and contested domains. In this report, we do not include discussion of these issues largely because of classification concerns. For additional information on some of the unclassified cyber challenges, see GAO, *Defense Department Cyber Efforts: DOD Faces Challenges in Its Cyber Activities*, GAO-11-75 (Washington, D.C.: July 25, 2011).

eventually inform Army assessments of capability needs, gaps, and solutions.

The Marine Corps has also incorporated consideration of A2/AD challenges into *Expeditionary Force 21*, its capstone concept, which provides guidance for how the Marine Corps will be organized, trained, and equipped to fulfill its assigned responsibilities over the next 10 years.[12] Published in March 2014, the concept identifies the JOAC as an input and is consistent with many of its themes, including the importance of distributed operations. *Expeditionary Force 21* identifies a number of challenges to Marine Corps operations caused by A2/AD threats and proposes a number of potential solutions for how the service will overcome them, including operating from amphibious ships farther from shore and using dispersed formations. According to Marine Corps officials, the service is also developing a number of supporting concepts, including some with the Navy that will further explore proposed approaches for overcoming A2/AD challenges. These officials stated that eventually this will inform Marine Corps assessments of capability needs, gaps, and solutions. The officials added that while the capstone concept has been issued and the associated analysis and innovation is under way, developing the full range of capabilities envisioned will be a long-term endeavor.

In addition, the Army and Marine Corps are incorporating operational access challenges into their wargames. Services conduct wargames for multiple reasons, including mission rehearsal, concept analysis, and doctrine validation. The Army's Unified Quest wargames explore a broad range of future conflicts and have included A2/AD scenarios. For example, the scenario for Unified Quest 2013 was set in the 2030-2040 time frame with fictional adversaries adopting hybrid warfighting approaches that used a mix of A2/AD capabilities, including integrated air defenses, cyber warfare, and anti-ship cruise missiles. The wargame explored new operating concepts, including how to effectively fight with dispersed forces. The Marine Corps' Expeditionary Warrior wargames have also included A2/AD challenges. For example, Expeditionary Warrior 2012 was set in 2024 in a fictional country where state and

---

[12]*Expeditionary Force 21* fits within the naval strategy as described by *A Cooperative Strategy for 21st Century Seapower*—U.S. Navy, U.S. Marine Corps, and U.S. Coast Guard, *A Cooperative Strategy for 21st Century Seapower* (Washington, D.C.: October 2007).

nonstate adversaries were armed with A2/AD capabilities, including cyber warfare, ballistic missiles, anti-ship cruise missiles, integrated air defense systems, mines, and submarines. The Marine Corps used this wargame, in part, to explore integration with special operations, cyber, and other joint forces.

Although they have functions important to overcoming the range of A2/AD challenges, the Army and Marine Corps have focused their wargames on A2/AD challenges from states and failed or failing states with less-advanced A2/AD capabilities. A primary reason for this approach, according to Army and Marine Corps officials, is that ground forces are likely to have a larger role in failed and failing state scenarios as compared with their roles in scenarios involving a peer or near-peer competitor. Further, such conflicts are more likely than a conflict with a peer competitor (see fig. 4). The officials added that the Army and Marine Corps participate in Navy and Air Force wargames that examine the A2/AD challenges posed by peer competitors.

Figure 4: Focus of Army and Marine Corps Wargame Scenarios

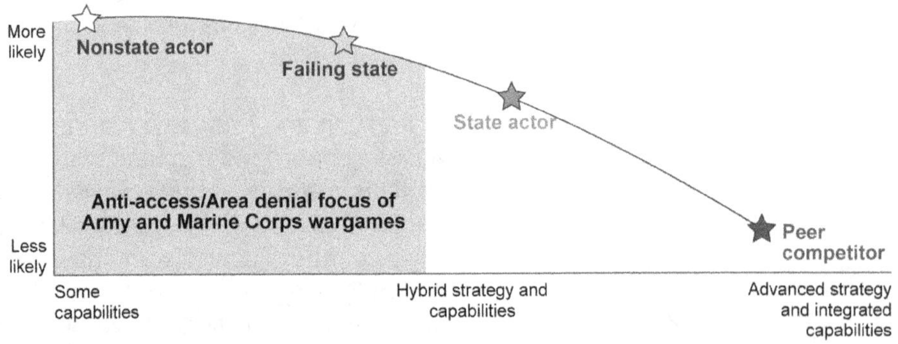

Source: GAO analysis of Department of Defense information. | GAO-14-801

Note: Not to scale.

Army and Marine Corps Have Identified Important Roles in Overcoming Operational Access Challenges and Are Beginning to Take Steps to Change How They Carry Out These Roles

Engagement Activities

The Army and the Marine Corps have identified several areas where they have important roles in overcoming operational access challenges. According to Army and Marine Corps officials, A2/AD challenges impact a broad range of their existing missions but do not create new ones.[13] While A2/AD challenges impact many missions, primary missions include the engagement activities and entry operations of both services, as well as logistics and missile defense for the Army. The services are beginning to take steps to change how they carry out these missions. Some of these efforts are expected to stretch well into the next decade and beyond.

The Army and the Marine Corps play a primary role in establishing access through their engagement activities and are using these opportunities to help address A2/AD challenges, according to DOD officials. The JOAC emphasizes that success in overcoming A2/AD challenges in combat often depends on activities prior to conflict that help gain and maintain access and identifies three required capabilities for such activities.[14] According to the JOAC, such activities include multinational exercises, basing and support agreements, improving overseas facilities, prepositioning supplies, and forward-deploying forces. These types of activities help shape favorable access conditions. For example, engagement activities such as combined training or exercises, or improving a host-nation's infrastructure, help maintain and develop good relationships with and improve the capabilities of allies and partners that then may be called upon in the event of a crisis. Also, officials from the U.S. Pacific Command (PACOM) and the U.S. Central Command (CENTCOM) emphasized the importance of engagement activities in gaining and maintaining access and stated that continued forward presence of U.S. forces in their regions may help deter potential adversaries and reassure allies and partners by signaling U.S. commitment to that region.[15] Moreover, DOD officials stated that having

---

[13]Public law and DOD guidance identify the roles and functions of the services, including the Army and the Marine Corps, see United States Code, Title 10, section 3062 for the Army and section 5063 for the Marine Corps, and DODD 5100.01 (Dec. 21, 2010).

[14]See app. I, capability numbers 28, 29, and 30.

[15]DOD has nine combatant commands with an assigned geographic region or assigned function. The six geographic commands, which have defined areas of operation and have a distinct regional military focus, are U.S. Africa Command, U.S. Central Command, U.S. European Command, U.S. Northern Command, U.S. Pacific Command, and U.S. Southern Command. The three functional commands, which have unique capabilities and operate worldwide, are U.S. Special Operations Command, U.S. Strategic Command, and U.S. Transportation Command.

Army and Marine Corps forces forward deployed conducting engagement activities helps with access challenges because these forces are already in theater and can respond more quickly if a crisis occurs than they could if they had to deploy from the United States.

Both the Army and Marine Corps are developing new approaches to their engagement activities to help shape favorable access conditions. For example, the Army is testing a new operational approach in 2014, called Pacific Pathways, that changes the way the Army supplies forces for engagement activities. Rather than sending a number of small units that each conduct a single activity for a short period of time, under Pacific Pathways the Army will send a fully-equipped, combat-trained, 700-soldier battalion-sized force to participate in two or three regional exercises over the course of 90 days. Soldiers and their equipment would travel by air and sea between engagements. Similarly, the Marine Corps is also taking steps to enhance engagement activities and provide forward presence. The Marine Corps is planning on having one-third of its forces forward deployed. As part of this effort, the Marine Corps is returning to the practice of rotational deployments, where units based in the United States deploy to Japan or Australia for 6 months to train, engage allies and partners in the region, and provide forward presence. According to DOD officials, these approaches allow the forces to better fulfill their respective missions while providing the combatant commanders with more options for their employment.

In addition, officials from CENTCOM, PACOM, and U.S. Special Operations Command told us they are increasingly incorporating engagement activities into their planning efforts. Moreover, the JOAC states that combatant commanders will need to coordinate these efforts with other U.S. agencies that are also conducting engagement activities. In February 2013, we testified that as DOD continues to emphasize engagement activities, to include building partner capacity, the need for efficient and effective coordination with foreign partners and within the U.S. government has become more important, in part because of fiscal challenges, which can be exacerbated by overlapping or ineffective efforts.[16]

---

[16]GAO, *Building Partner Capacity: Key Practices to Effectively Manage Department of Defense Efforts to Promote Security Cooperation*, GAO-13-335T (Washington, D.C.: Feb. 14, 2013). This testimony summarized the results of a body of work we have conducted on DOD's efforts in this area.

Entry Operations	The Army and the Marine Corps both play a primary role in conducting entry operations in an A2/AD environment, according to DOD. Entry operations are the projection and immediate employment of military forces from the sea or through the air onto foreign territory to accomplish assigned missions.[17] The JOAC states that maintaining or expanding operational access may require entry of Army or Marine Corps forces into hostile territory to accomplish missions, such as eliminating land-based threats or initiating sustained land operations, and identifies the ability to conduct forcible entry operations as a required capability.

The Army has conducted several studies, exercises, and wargames that examine entry operations in an A2/AD environment and concluded, among other things, that it must be able to deploy decisive force much more rapidly. The Army identified a number of areas requiring improvement, including enhancing engagement with friends and allies, increasing the ability to deploy small units, reducing logistics demands, and greatly advancing technologies such as vertical lift, lighter yet survivable vehicles, missile defenses, and command and control. Moreover, for Army airborne units, the Army has identified the need for capabilities such as weapon systems and vehicles that can be air-dropped in a location and provide forces with long-range, precision firepower; mobility across a range of terrain; and protection, among other things.[18] It has further outlined an approach intended to achieve some improvements by 2025 and to have significantly improved forces in the 2040 time frame.

The Marine Corps is also examining how to conduct entry operations in an A2/AD environment. According to the Marine Corps, the joint force has become brittle and risk averse because of its reliance on a small number of very advanced and expensive weapons systems that are increasingly vulnerable to A2/AD capabilities. A key force priority for overcoming A2/AD challenges is resilience, according to PACOM officials. To increase resilience, the Marine Corps is developing the idea of using a greater number of highly mobile capabilities on expeditionary advanced bases—small, temporary, austere, and distributed bases that can be established for a variety of purposes. For example, the Marine Corps

---

[17]*Joint Concept for Entry Operations* working definition of entry operations.

[18]The Army refers to these capabilities as mobile protected firepower and enhanced mobility for airborne infantry.

could use land-based anti-ship missiles on small mobile platforms to control sea-lanes. However, according to the Marine Corps, pursuing this idea would require it to obtain new missile capabilities as well as more flexible supply and command and control systems than are currently in place. Additionally, the Marine Corps is examining operating short-takeoff/vertical-landing-capable joint strike fighters from small distributed bases; however, according to the Marine Corps, it has not yet determined the supportability requirements for this aircraft in austere environments. The Marine Corps is aware of such challenges and is in the early stages of addressing them. It has not yet completed the concepts and follow-on analyses needed to support the implementation of these ideas, according to Marine Corps officials.

Logistics

The Army has a fundamental role in providing logistics support in an A2/AD environment, according to DOD, and the JOAC states that increased threats and operational demands of future operations in such environments may present challenges for logistics.[19] Specifically, the JOAC states that logistics hubs and networks may be increasingly vulnerable to attack by adversaries with A2/AD capabilities, such as cyber, counterspace, and ballistic missiles. Further, one of DOD's and the Army's approaches to conducting operations in an A2/AD environment is to use multiple smaller units operating independently, but supporting such units is more logistically demanding. The JOAC identifies three required capabilities for logistics, but also notes that new logistics concepts are needed to explore the challenges to logistics in an A2/AD environment and to help define required capabilities. Also, a study examining the impacts of the JOAC on joint logistics echoed this need.[20] According to

---

[19]Our prior body of work has also identified challenges associated with logistics. Specifically, DOD's management of its supply chain has been included in GAO's biennial high-risk report since 1990. While DOD has demonstrated top leadership support and has directed time and resources for improving supply chain management, several long-standing problems have not yet been resolved. These problems relate to DOD's ability to manage its inventory, to maintain visibility over its materiel and assets, and to assess the overall effectiveness of its supply chain across the department. GAO, *High-Risk Series: An Update*, GAO-13-283 (Washington, D.C.: Feb. 14, 2013).

[20]U.S. Transportation Command, *Future Deployment and Distribution Assessment: Joint Operational Access Concept*, A-5CFB2F1 (Sept. 25, 2012).

GAO-14-801 Defense Planning

officials from the Joint Staff and the Army, they have begun revising the *Joint Concept for Logistics*, in part, to include A2/AD challenges.[21]

In addition, the Army is examining how it might address A2/AD challenges related to logistics. One way that the Army is proposing to mitigate the problem of increased demands on logistics is to focus efforts on decreasing the Army's and the joint force's demand for items such as fuel, water, and ammunition. For example, the Army's *Functional Concept for Sustainment*, issued in October 2010, states that during operations in Iraq, 22 percent of all convoys into the theater per year were for fuel. The concept states that technological advances are needed to reduce the fuel demand for vehicles and energy production, among other things. In addition, the Army is exploring unmanned distribution of supplies in theater to help provide timely sustainment and reduce the exposure of soldiers to potential threats. A 2013 Army Unified Quest wargame report stated that while this technology could provide benefits, additional study is needed to understand how and when automated systems should be used, as well as the costs, such as those for maintenance, that would be involved.

Missile Defense

Another primary Army contribution to overcoming A2/AD challenges is providing active missile defenses, according to DOD. The JOAC notes that the increasing accuracy, lethality, and proliferation of ballistic and cruise missiles are a key A2/AD challenge. Further, such capabilities are attractive to potential adversaries because they are cost imposing: that is, defenses against ballistic and cruise missiles tend to be more costly than the missiles themselves. According to DOD, adversaries will use ballistic and cruise missiles to counter U.S. power projection capabilities by attacking forward bases, naval forces, and logistics support and command and control capabilities. The JOAC therefore identifies expeditionary missile defense as a required capability for overcoming access challenges.

Land-based missile defense is a core Army function and a main element of DOD's force structure, according to DOD. Although the JOAC does not

---

[21]Joint Staff, *Joint Concept for Logistics*, (Washington, D.C.: Aug. 6, 2010). The 2010 *Joint Concept for Logistics* describes a vision of what logistics support needs to look like in the 2016-2028 time frame across the basic categories of military activities, such as combat, security, engagement, and relief and reconstruction activities. According to Joint Staff officials, the published version does not consider A2/AD challenges.

provide a clear definition of what constitutes expeditionary missile defense, several characteristics of the Army's missile defense force structure indicate that they do not meet this required capability, including the following:

- Mobility/supportability—The JOAC emphasizes the need for smaller and highly mobile systems requiring little support. Current Army missile defenses are transportable but lack strategic and tactical mobility, according to the Army. They also have large logistical requirements.[22]

- Capacity—According to DOD, demand for missile defenses, including those provided by the Army, exceeds capacity. Missiles are the core of adversary A2/AD capabilities, and growing adversary missile inventories and improving capabilities will exacerbate capacity issues.[23]

- Cost—According to DOD, current missile defenses are very expensive. By pursuing increasingly advanced missiles, adversaries are able to impose costs on the United States.

Army and Army-sponsored reviews recognize some of these difficulties and have recommended that more attention be paid to other, less costly technologies that can protect against large numbers of missiles, such as directed energy weapons and railguns.[24] DOD's Strategic Capabilities Office is working with the Navy and others to develop a railgun that can provide cost-effective land-based ballistic and cruise missile defense

---

[22]In April 2014, we reported that the Army and the Missile Defense Agency had not yet determined the long-term support strategy for the Terminal High-Altitude Area Defense. The 2014 QDR identifies the Terminal High-Altitude Area Defense as a major component of the Army's force structure in 2019. See GAO, *Ballistic Missile Defense: Actions Needed to Address Implementation Issues and Estimate Long-Term Costs for European Capabilities*, GAO-14-314 (Washington, D.C.: Apr. 11, 2014).

[23]In January 2011, we reported that DOD had not established key operational performance metrics that would provide the combatant commands with needed visibility into the operational capabilities and limitations of the ballistic missile defense system they intend to employ. See GAO, *Ballistic Missile Defense: DOD Needs to Address Planning and Implementation Challenges for Future Capabilities in Europe*, GAO-11-220 (Washington, D.C.: Jan. 26, 2011).

[24]Directed energy weapons use a beam of concentrated electromagnetic energy or atomic or subatomic particles to incapacitate, damage, or destroy enemy equipment, facilities, or personnel. An electromagnetic railgun is a long-range weapon that fires a projectile using electricity instead of chemical propellants.

capability.[25] They are also investigating how DOD could combine railgun projectiles with sensors and existing guns, including Army artillery, to shoot down cruise missiles. These alternatives could provide high-capacity, cost-effective missile defense capabilities, but they have not yet matured into programs, according to the Strategic Capabilities Office. According to the Army, power generation, storage, and mobility issues associated with directed energy weapons and railguns will be resolved in the 2040 time frame.

DOD Is in the Early Stages of Developing the JOAC Implementation Plan, but Has Not Fully Established Specific Measures and Milestones to Assess Progress

DOD is developing an implementation plan for the JOAC in order to bring coherence to the department's many simultaneous efforts to overcome A2/AD challenges but has not fully established measures and milestones to gauge progress.[26] The Joint Staff is leading a multiyear DOD-wide effort to coordinate, oversee, and assess the department's implementation of the JOAC. DOD is planning to issue the first iteration of the plan in 2014 and intends to assess and update the plan annually. However, the draft 2014 JOAC Implementation Plan is limited in scope and does not fully establish the specific measures and milestones DOD needs to allow decision makers to assess the progress the department is making, including the contributions of the Army and the Marine Corps.

DOD Is in the Early Stages of Developing the Joint Operational Access Concept Implementation Plan

The Joint Staff is leading a multiyear DOD-wide effort, initiated in June 2013, to coordinate, oversee, and assess the department's implementation of the JOAC. In order for DOD to fulfill its mission to *project power despite A2/AD challenges*, the 2012 Defense Strategic Guidance requires DOD to implement the JOAC. In addition, DOD guidance on concept development requires DOD to develop and execute implementation plans for joint concepts and to assess their

---

[25]The Strategic Capabilities Office was established in August 2012 by the Under Secretary of Defense for Acquisition, Technology, and Logistics in order to provide cost-effective, strategic alternatives to shape and counter emerging threats by leveraging existing concepts, systems, and technologies in unique and innovative ways.

[26]For purposes of this report, we use the term "JOAC Implementation Plan," however, DOD refers to the implementation plan for the JOAC as the "Joint Operational Access Implementation Plan." Officials use this term because the plan will cover the JOAC and other supporting concepts, such as the *Joint Concept for Entry Operations*.

implementation.[27] The guidance was issued in November 2013 and the JOAC is the first joint concept to be implemented under the new guidance, according to DOD officials. They further stated that the emphasis on implementation is a significant and positive change to the guidance but will be challenging to execute.

In accordance with this guidance, DOD is planning to issue the first iteration of the JOAC Implementation Plan in August 2014 and intends to assess and update the plan annually.[28] Previously, DOD did not have a single place where it was tracking and coordinating its efforts to address A2/AD challenges, including those of the Army and Marine Corps, even though the JOAC notes that addressing A2/AD challenges requires closer integration between services than ever before. The draft 2014 JOAC Implementation Plan states that it is intended to provide coherence by integrating, overseeing, communicating, and assessing the various efforts being taken across DOD to create the capabilities required to overcome A2/AD challenges.[29]

A working group, led by the Joint Staff and with representatives from stakeholders across the department, including the services and combatant commands, drafted the 2014 implementation plan. The development of the implementation plan was coordinated through the Joint Staff to ensure it was consistent with established processes, such as the Chairman's Capability Gap Assessment, according to Joint Staff

---

[27]Chairman of the Joint Chiefs of Staff Instruction (CJCSI) 3010.02D, *Guidance for Development and Implementation of Joint Concepts*, (Washington, D.C.: Nov. 22, 2013).

[28]The first iteration of the implementation plan—the 2014 plan—remains in draft as of July 2014.

[29]The JOAC Implementation Plan has four specific purposes: (1) develop a comprehensive, DOD understanding of ongoing JOAC implementation activities, (2) identify opportunities for joint collaboration to solve potential shortfalls in development efforts or eliminate duplicative activities, (3) establish a set of prioritized and approved recommendations for implementation of materiel and nonmateriel solutions in order to increase focus and integrate efforts to address critical challenges, and (4) provide comprehensive assessments to military decision makers on progress toward the development of required capabilities.

officials.[30] These officials stated that the intent was to leverage existing force development processes to gather information about current and planned activities that contributed to the implementation of the JOAC. They further noted that the JOAC implementation process may eventually address not only capability issues but also capacity issues, which officials from the Army, Marine Corps, and the combatant commands we spoke with noted were critical in terms of overcoming A2/AD challenges.

Because of the large scope of the JOAC and to help familiarize stakeholders with a new process, Joint Staff officials stated that the working group decided to focus the first iteration of the plan on 10 required capabilities that it determined to be the highest priority rather than including all 30 JOAC-required capabilities.[31] Once those capabilities were identified, officials said that working group members, including those from the Army and Marine Corps, reviewed ongoing and planned activities from their respective organizations that they believed would align with the implementation of 1 or more of the 10 prioritized capabilities.

Joint Staff officials said that they also conducted a supplemental review of published planning documents to identify any further relevant planned implementation actions. These efforts resulted in an execution matrix containing 165 discrete implementation actions that include nonmateriel solutions, such as changes in doctrine and testing concepts in wargames or experiments, as well as materiel solutions, such as buying a piece of equipment. According to the draft plan, approximately 88 percent of the actions were nonmateriel. Each action included a recommended timeline

---

[30]The Capability Gap Assessment is a Joint Staff process that examines identified capability gaps and shortfalls in the current force from various perspectives, groups together "like" gaps, assesses ongoing efforts to close or mitigate capability gaps, and recommends solutions to close or mitigate capability gaps. The result of the assessment is a list, for Joint Requirements Oversight Council approval, of capability gaps and recommended solutions for mitigation.

[31]The JOAC identifies 30 required capabilities as essential to the implementation of the concept (see app. I). While the 30 capabilities are unclassified, when they are ordered in terms of priority, they become classified. Thus, the 10 capabilities that were considered the highest priority for the department are classified. The working group identified the 10 priorities by comparing DOD's current list of prioritized gaps in the Chairman's Capability Gap Assessment with the list of JOAC capabilities. The working group also included a special topic in the annual Chairman's Joint Assessment that asked the services, combatant commanders, and other DOD organizations to identify the highest-priority JOAC-required capabilities.

for completion determined by the organization responsible for the action that could span several years. Thus, for each capability, multiple organizations are simultaneously undertaking implementation actions with various timelines for completion. Joint Staff officials stated that the execution matrix revealed that DOD was already taking many actions addressing the 10 prioritized capabilities.

Officials noted that the 165 implementation actions do not constitute the full effort required to complete implementation of these 10 required capabilities, and future iterations of the execution matrix will be updated as required based on analyses to identify additional discrete implementation actions. In addition, future iterations of the JOAC Implementation Plan will also include the other JOAC-required capabilities as well as required capabilities from other joint concepts that support the JOAC, according to Joint Staff officials.[32]

Draft Implementation Plan Does Not Have Fully Established Specific Measures and Milestones to Assess Progress

The draft 2014 JOAC Implementation Plan does not fully establish the specific measures and milestones DOD needs to allow decision makers to assess the progress the department is making, including the contributions of the Army and the Marine Corps. DOD guidance requires that all joint concepts have an implementation plan that includes measures and milestones that allow decision makers to gauge implementation progress.[33] Further, a stated purpose of the plan is to measure progress toward the development of a joint force able to project power despite A2/AD challenges. Internal control standards in the federal government also call for agencies to provide reasonable assurance to decision makers that their objectives are being achieved and that decision makers have reliable data to determine whether they are meeting goals and using resources effectively and efficiently.[34] Moreover, GAO's

---

[32]Currently, there are two supporting concepts, the Joint Concept for Entry Operations and the Air-Sea Battle Concept. Officials stated that there are several other supporting concepts that are being drafted, such as the Joint Concept for Rapid Aggregation. However, there are no current plans to include the Air-Sea Battle Concept in the implementation plan for the JOAC. While the Air-Sea Battle Concept is considered to be a supporting concept to the JOAC, it was issued before the JOAC, and the Air Sea Battle Office has developed its own implementation plan for the former. Joint Staff and Air Sea Battle Office officials stated that the two implementation plans may merge in the future.

[33]CJCSI 3010.02D.

[34]GAO/AIMD-00-21.3.1

Schedule Assessment Guide states that milestones and measures are essential for tracking an organization's progress toward achieving intermediate and long-term goals, and helping to identify critical phases of the project and the essential activities needed to be completed within given time frames.[35]

The draft JOAC Implementation Plan identifies four stages at which the working group is to assess implementation.

- *Implementation Actions.* The working group is to assess the progress made in implementing the discrete materiel and nonmateriel actions in the execution matrix.

- *Required Capabilities.* The working group is to assess progress in implementing each JOAC-required capability based on the progress made on completing the implementation actions relevant to that capability.

- *Operational Objectives.* The Implementation Plan organizes the required capabilities into four operational objectives—the broad goals a commander must achieve in order to project power despite A2/AD challenges.[36] The working group is to assess progress in implementing each operational objective based on the progress of the required capabilities aligned under each objective.

- *End State.* The working group is to assess progress in reaching the JOAC end state based on the implementation progress of the four operational objectives.

The draft 2014 JOAC Implementation Plan includes measures and milestones for the 165 identified implementation actions but not for the other three implementation stages. Specifically, the 165 actions will be assessed as being either complete or not yet complete, according to Joint

---

[35]GAO-12-120G

[36]The four operational objectives are to (1) gain and maintain cooperative regional advantage; (2) aggregate the force; (3) disrupt, destroy, and defeat A2/AD; and (4) conduct sustained operations. These operational objectives are similar to the first four phases of war—Phase 0 (shape), Phase 1 (deter), Phase 2 (seize initiative), and Phase 3 (dominate). Joint Staff officials stated that they did not use these phases because a commander may need to take action to address each objective simultaneously or in varying order. See Chairman, Joint Chiefs of Staff, Joint Publication 5-0, *Joint Operational Planning* (Washington, D.C.: Aug. 11, 2011).

Staff officials. However, Joint Staff officials stated the working group has not yet developed the necessary measures to gauge the extent to which required capabilities, operational objectives, or the end state have been implemented. For example, the working group has not yet developed measures for how the completion of an implementation action affects the completion of the required capability to which it is tied. In other words, the aggregate of the implementation actions will show how much work has been completed—i.e., the number of actions—but it will not show how much work remains to be completed to fully implement the required capability. Thus, even if DOD completed all 165 implementation actions identified in the first plan, it currently would not be able to determine the progress in implementing the 10 required capabilities. Figure 5 shows the stages at which the draft 2014 JOAC Implementation Plan has measures and milestones.

Figure 5: Draft 2014 Joint Operational Access Concept Implementation Plan Measures and Milestones

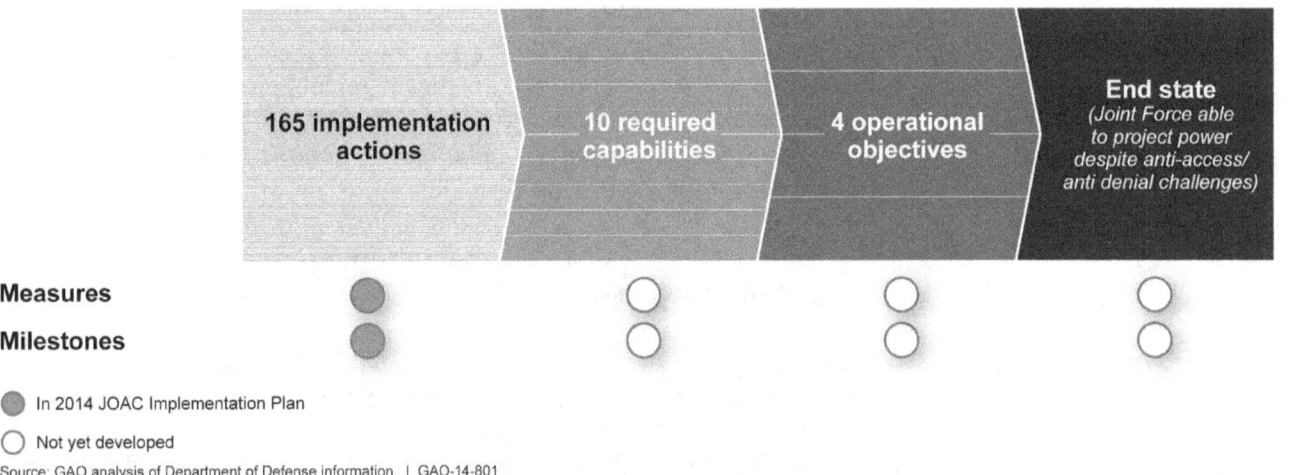

Source: GAO analysis of Department of Defense information. | GAO-14-801

Similarly, the draft 2014 JOAC Implementation Plan does not fully identify milestones for all four implementation stages. Specifically, the plan identifies milestones for the 165 implementation actions, but not for required capabilities, operational objectives, and the end state. Moreover, the 2014 plan does not indicate if or when milestones will be established. For example, the implementation plan does not identify when the required capability for expeditionary missile defense should be completed, and Army officials told us that plans for developing this high-priority capability may take decades. Additionally, the plan does not identify milestones for implementing the operational objective related to engagement activities, which, as noted previously, is an area in which the Army and Marine Corps play primary roles.

Joint Staff officials emphasized that the 2014 JOAC Implementation Plan is the first of many iterations and was intended only to provide visibility of ongoing activities relevant to the top 10 JOAC-required capabilities. Joint Staff officials stated that they intend to include ways to assess overall implementation progress in future iterations of the plan. Specifically, the draft 2014 Implementation Plan states that the working group will establish a process to aggregate implementation actions in such a way as to allow it to gauge progress at the required capability, operational objective, and end state stages. However, the draft plan provides no detail about how or when this will be accomplished.

While DOD has stated its intent to assess progress in the future, its current planning lacks specifics about the measures it will employ and how it will set milestones to gauge that progress. Consequently, the draft 2014 plan is not fully consistent with DOD guidance, as well as federal internal control standards and GAO's *Schedule Assessment Guide*, that emphasize the importance of tracking an organization's progress toward achieving its goals. Without establishing specific measures and milestones in future iterations of the JOAC Implementation Plan, DOD will not be able to gauge JOAC implementation progress and assess whether efforts by the joint force, to include the Army and the Marine Corps, will achieve DOD's goals in desired time frames in the near and long terms. Specifically, if DOD does not have a means to assess implementation progress, it may lack assurance that Army and Marine Corps efforts to address areas such as engagement activities, entry operations, logistics support, and expeditionary missile defense fully align with the JOAC. Moreover, without an effective implementation plan that allows decision makers to track progress over time, DOD will not have the assurance that it will be able to provide commanders with the forces they need to overcome A2/AD challenges envisioned to be faced by the joint force of 2020.

Conclusions

The proliferation of relatively low-cost advanced technologies and the emergence of space and cyberspace as contested domains, along with the change in U.S. overseas defense posture, present DOD with a future operational environment that no longer includes the unimpeded operational access DOD has enjoyed for decades. As potential adversaries develop strategies aimed at preventing the U.S. military from arriving at the fight and complicating its freedom of action once there, DOD's planning has shifted to focus on how to maintain its ability to project power into operational areas. While DOD may have initially emphasized the role of the Air Force and Navy in overcoming A2/AD challenges, the Army and the Marine Corps also have primary roles to play and are beginning to address these challenges.

DOD's effort to develop an implementation plan is a significant step and provides the foundation for a roadmap to move the JOAC from concept to implementation. However, since it does not yet include specific measures and milestones that would allow DOD to gauge JOAC implementation progress, it is not yet clear the extent to which efforts across the department to address A2/AD challenges, including those of the Army and Marine Corps, support JOAC implementation, or whether current efforts align with JOAC implementation time frames. Given that some of the department's efforts to address JOAC-required capabilities, such as the Army's work on missile defense, may take many years, a means to assess progress is essential. Specifically, fully establishing measures and milestones would clarify what additional steps the Army and Marine Corps may need to take to align their current efforts to address A2/AD challenges—including with respect to their key roles in engagement activities, entry operations, logistics support, and missile defense—with the required capabilities in the JOAC. Until future iterations of the JOAC Implementation Plan contain specific measures and milestones to gauge progress, DOD may find it difficult to judge whether it is on target to meet its overall goal of ensuring the joint force of 2020 can operate effectively in an A2/AD environment.

Recommendation for Executive Action

To improve DOD's ability to assess *Joint Operational Access Concept* implementation, including the contribution of the Army and the Marine Corps, we recommend that the Secretary of Defense direct the Joint Staff, in coordination with the Army, the Marine Corps, and other members of the working group, to establish specific measures and milestones in future iterations of the JOAC Implementation Plan to gauge how individual implementation actions contribute in the near and long terms to achieving the required capabilities, operational objectives, and end state envisioned by the department.

Agency Comments and Our Evaluation

We provided a draft of this report to DOD for review and comment. DOD provided written comments, which are summarized below and reprinted in appendix II. In its written comments, DOD partially concurred with the report's recommendation to establish specific measures and milestones in future iterations of the JOAC Implementation Plan to gauge how individual implementation actions contribute in the near and long term to achieving the required capabilities, operational objectives, and end state envisioned by the department.

In its comments, the department stated that it had previously recognized the need to assess JOAC implementation progress and that it had already begun to develop specific measures and milestones and would incorporate them into annual updates of the JOAC Implementation Plan. We noted in the report that DOD intended to include ways to assess overall implementation progress in future iterations of the implementation plan but that the draft 2014 plan did not fully establish specific measures and milestones to assess progress or provide detail for how progress would be assessed or when this would be accomplished. As also noted in the report, it is important that specific measures and milestones move beyond being able to assess progress of individual implementation actions and expand to allow the department to gauge JOAC implementation progress and assess whether efforts by the joint force, to include the Army and the Marine Corps, will achieve DOD's goals in desired time frames in the near and long terms. In doing so, DOD will be better positioned to judge whether it is on target to meet its overall goal of ensuring the joint force of 2020 can operate effectively in an A2/AD environment.

DOD also provided technical comments, which we have incorporated as appropriate.

We are sending copies of this report to appropriate congressional committees, the Secretary of Defense, the Chairman of the Joint Chiefs of Staff, the Secretary of the Army, and the Commandant of the Marine Corps. In addition, the report is available at no charge on the GAO website at http://www.gao.gov.

If you or your staff have any questions about this report, please contact me at (202) 512-3489 or pendletonj@gao.gov. Contact points for our Offices of Congressional Relations and Public Affairs may be found on the last page of this report. GAO staff who made key contributions to this report are listed in appendix III.

John H. Pendleton

Director
Defense Capabilities and Management

List of Committees

The Honorable Carl Levin
Chairman
The Honorable James M. Inhofe
Ranking Member
Committee on Armed Services
United States Senate

The Honorable Richard J. Durbin
Chairman
The Honorable Thad Cochran
Ranking Member
Subcommittee on Defense
Committee on Appropriations
United States Senate

The Honorable Howard P. "Buck" McKeon
Chairman
The Honorable Adam Smith
Ranking Member
Committee on Armed Services
House of Representatives

The Honorable Rodney Frelinghuysen
Chairman
The Honorable Peter J. Visclosky
Ranking Member
Subcommittee on Defense
Committee on Appropriations
House of Representatives

Appendix I: Joint Operational Access Concept Required Capabilities

The *Joint Operational Access Concept* (JOAC) identifies 30 capabilities considered essential to the implementation of the concept and what the future joint force will need to gain operational access in an opposed environment. According to the JOAC, the list of required capabilities is neither complete nor prioritized but provides a baseline for further analysis and concept development. The JOAC organizes the required capabilities in eight categories as described below.

Command and Control

1. The ability to maintain reliable connectivity and interoperability among major warfighting headquarters and supported/supporting forces while en route.

2. The ability to perform effective command and control in a degraded and/or austere communications environment.

3. The ability to create sharable, user-defined operating pictures from a common database to provide situational awareness (including friendly, enemy, and neutral situations) across the domains.

4. The ability to integrate cross-domain operations, to include at lower echelons, with the full integration of space and cyberspace operations.

5. The ability to employ mission command to enable subordinate commanders to act independently in consonance with the higher commander's intent and effect the necessary cross-domain integration laterally at the required echelon.

Intelligence

6. The ability of operational forces to detect and respond to hostile computer network attack in an opposed access situation.

7. The ability to conduct timely and accurate cross-domain all-source intelligence fusion in an opposed access situation.

8. The ability to develop all categories of intelligence in any necessary domain in the context of opposed access.

Fires

9. The ability to locate, target, and suppress or neutralize hostile anti-access and area denial capabilities in complex terrain with the necessary range, precision, responsiveness, and reversible and permanent effects while limiting collateral damage.

10. The ability to leverage cross-domain cueing to detect and engage in-depth to delay, disrupt, or destroy enemy systems.

11. The ability to conduct electronic attack and computer network attack against hostile anti-access/area denial capabilities.

12. The ability to interdict enemy forces and materiel deploying to an operational area.

Movement and Maneuver

13. The ability to conduct and support operational maneuver over strategic distances along multiple axes of advance by air and sea.

14. The ability to "maneuver" in cyberspace to gain entry into hostile digital networks.

15. The ability to conduct en route command and control, mission planning and rehearsal, and assembly of deploying forces, to include linking up of personnel and prepositioned equipment.

16. The ability to conduct forcible entry operations, from raids and other limited-objective operations to the initiation of sustained land operations.

17. The ability to mask the approach of joint maneuver elements to enable those forces to penetrate sophisticated anti-access systems and close within striking range with acceptable risk.

Protection

18. The ability to defeat enemy targeting systems, including their precision firing capabilities.

19. The ability to provide expeditionary missile defense to counter the increased precision, lethality, and range of enemy anti-access/area denial systems.

20. The ability to protect and, if necessary, reconstitute bases and other infrastructure required to project military force, to include points of origin, ports of embarkation and debarkation, and intermediate staging bases.

21. The ability to protect forces and supplies deploying by sea and air.

22. The ability to protect friendly space forces while disrupting enemy space operations.

23. The ability to conduct cyber defense in the context of opposed access.

Sustainment

24. The ability to deploy, employ, and sustain forces via a global network of fixed and mobile bases, to include seabasing.

25. The ability to quickly and flexibly establish nonstandard support mechanisms, such as the use of commercial providers and facilities.

26. The ability to plan, manage, and integrate contractor support in the context of operations to gain operational access in the face of armed resistance.

Information

27. The ability to inform and influence selected audiences to facilitate operational access before, during, and after hostilities.

Engagement

28. The ability to develop relationships and partnership goals and to share capabilities and capacities to ensure access and advance long-term regional stability.

29. The ability to secure basing, navigation, and overflight rights and support agreements from regional partners.

30. The ability to provide training, supplies, equipment, and other assistance to regional partners to improve their access capabilities.

Appendix II: Comments from the Department of Defense

OFFICE OF THE UNDER SECRETARY OF DEFENSE
2000 DEFENSE PENTAGON
WASHINGTON, D.C. 20301-2000

POLICY

Mr. John H. Pendleton
Director, Defense Capabilities and Management
U.S. Government Accountability Office
441 G. Street, NW
Washington, DC 20548

Dear Mr. Pendleton:

This is the Department of Defense response to the Government Accountability Office (GAO) draft report GAO-14-801, "DOD Needs Specific Measures and Milestones to Gauge Progress of Preparations for Operational Access Challenges," dated September 2014 (GAO Code 351833). The Department partially concurs with the recommendation in the report (see Enclosure A for details). The GAO report indicates, and the Department agrees, that it is important to assess the progress of the Joint Operational Access Concept Implementation Plan. The Department notes that it had already begun developing specific measures and milestones within the Implementation Plan, as recommended by the GAO, and will continue to refine these tracking tools in the future.

The Department appreciates the opportunity to respond to your draft report. We look forward to your continued cooperation and dialogue toward improving ongoing and future work to prepare for operational access challenges. Should you have any questions, please contact Col Bill Vivian, (703) 697-4001, william.h.vivian.mil@mail.mil.

Sincerely,

Robert M. Scher
Acting Deputy Under Secretary of Defense for
Strategy, Plans, and Forces

GAO DRAFT REPORT DATED JULY 31, 2014
GAO-14-801 (GAO CODE 351833)

"DEFENSE PLANNING: DOD NEEDS SPECIFIC MEASURES AND
MILESTONES TO GAUGE PROGRESS OF PREPARATIONS FOR
OPERATIONAL ACCESS CHALLENGES"

DEPARTMENT OF DEFENSE COMMENTS
TO THE GAO RECOMMENDATION

RECOMMENDATION: The GAO recommends the following: "To improve DoD's ability to assess Joint Operational Access implementation, including the contribution of the Army and the Marine Corps, we recommend that the Secretary of Defense direct the Joint Staff, in coordination with the Army, the Marine Corps, and other members of the working group, to establish specific measures and milestones in future iterations of the JOAC Implementation Plan to gauge how individual implementation actions contribute in the near and long term to achieving the required capabilities, operational objectives, and end state envisioned by the department."

DoD RESPONSE: The Department partially concurs with the GAO recommendation. As GAO notes in the report, DoD's effort to develop an implementation plan is a significant step and provides the foundation for executing the JOAC concept. The GAO helpfully observed that implementation would be aided by specific measures and milestones. The Department, in line with the GAO recommendations, had previously recognized the need to assess progress as the concept is implemented and consequently, had already begun to develop specific measures and milestones to track this progress that will be incorporated in annual updates to the JOAC Implementation Plan.

Appendix III: GAO Contact and Staff Acknowledgments

GAO Contact

John H. Pendleton, (202) 512-3489 or pendletonj@gao.gov

Staff Acknowledgments

In addition to the contact named above, Patricia Lentini, Assistant Director; Margaret Morgan, Assistant Director; Carolynn Cavanaugh; Colin Chambers; Nicolaas Cornelisse; Amie Steele; and Erik Wilkins-McKee made key contributions to this report.